The Trojan War

Sculptures by Anthony Caro

Photography by
David Buckland

Texts by
John Spurling and
Julius Bryant

Lund Humphries, London
in association with English Heritage
and Yorkshire Sculpture Park

First published in Great Britain in 1994 by
Lund Humphries Publishers Limited
Park House, 1 Russell Gardens
London NW11 9NN
in association with
English Heritage and Yorkshire Sculpture Park

to accompany the exhibition
THE TROJAN WAR: SCULPTURES BY ANTHONY CARO
at The Iveagh Bequest, Kenwood, London (English Heritage)
6 March to 6 April 1994
and Yorkshire Sculpture Park, Bretton Hall,
West Bretton, Wakefield, West Yorkshire
November 1994

British Library Cataloguing in Publication Data
A catalogue record for this book is available from
the British Library

ISBN 0 85331 663 5

Designed by Alan Bartram
Made and printed in Great Britain
by BAS Printers Limited
Over Wallop, Hampshire

ENGLISH HERITAGE

The London Historic House Museums Trust

Contents

Acknowledgements
Everyone involved in the *Trojan War* project has worked
enthusiastically and tirelessly.
In particular I would like to thank:

Hans Spinner, ceramicist, Grasse
Julius Bryant, English Heritage, Kenwood
Peter Murray, Yorkshire Sculpture Park
John Spurling, writer
David Buckland, photographer
John Taylor and Lucy Myers, Lund Humphries
Alan Bartram, designer
BAS Printers
Ian Barker, Annely Juda Gallery
Erica Bolton, Bolton and Quinn
The London Historic House Museums Trust, sponsors
Studio: Patrick Cunningham, Sue Brown, Derek Haworth,
Shapwick McDonnell, Michael Bolus, Ian Bettinson, Gavin
O'Curry, Sheila Girling
Hephaistos, god of fire

ANTHONY CARO

Caro's Trojan War
Julius Bryant

The Trojan War is among the most enduring and influential stories in Western culture. The siege of a small town on the north-west coast of Asia-Minor may or may not have happened, but over 3000 years later the tale of Helen, 'the face that launched a thousand ships', Achilles and the Trojan Horse, continues to fascinate. From the Greek epic poems of Homer to the paperbacks of Roger Lancelyn Green, the siege of Troy still rages, capturing the imaginations of new generations.

The challenge of interpreting the Trojan War is never the same, as all writers and artists bring to bear the interests of their own work and time, selecting and elaborating particular incidents, embellishing details or embracing the entire epic to help realise their highest ambitions and share their excitement. Two hundred years ago, during the neo-classical era, Homer ranked with Michelangelo as the essential standard and inspiration, particularly to British painters and sculptors. But in the twentieth century Homer's tale of the Trojan War, *The Iliad*, has been far from an artist's shelf of essential reading. In a century when subject-matter has seemed secondary to the artist's exploration of the qualities of materials, the expression of outlook and the abstract relation of shape, space, time and colour, characters from Greek myths have made only occasional appearances in contemporary art.[1] Despite these preoccupations, nearing the close of the century Anthony Caro has completed a group of thirty-eight sculptures exploring through three-dimensional composition the personalities of Homer's *Iliad*. Narrative, traditionally the prior concern of artists interpreting the epic, is left to the viewer, stepping through Caro's battlefield of abstract portraiture.

Before considering the immediate origins and ambitions behind Caro's *Trojan War* it is worth bringing an historical perspective to his new departure in order to explore past solutions, identify the qualities in Homer that appeal to artists, and the motivations that prompt them to portray particular subjects.

If Troy, situated east across the Aegean Sea from Greece in today's Turkey, ever fell, the favoured date is 1184 BC, an era of pre-Iron Age heroes, armed with leather body shields and bronze swords. Legends were passed on through oral tradition, recounting the tale of the ten-year siege by the Greek forces of the gateway to the East, elaborating the splendours of the merchant city, before one or more poets, believed by the Greeks themselves to be Homer, composed *The Iliad* and *The Odyssey*, probably in the eighth century BC. The chronicle would have been compiled for an upper-class Hellenic

Fig.1 Thomas Lawrence, *Homer Reciting his Poems*, 1790, oil on canvas, Tate Gallery.

audience keen to trace its ancestry from the war's heroes, for recital aloud, rather than silent solitary reading (see Fig.1).

The Iliad begins only in the tenth year of the war, describes a few weeks and ends before the fall of Troy, while *The Odyssey* tells the adventures of the survivors, particularly the ten-year journey home to Greece of Odysseus. For the complete story we are indebted to a group of post-Homeric poets who completed the Epic Cycle with a series of poems that used up the remaining source material, avoiding overlap with Homer's text. In the fifth century BC the Attic tragedians Sophocles, Euripides and Aeschylus expanded episodes and continued the narrative, and later writers, particularly the Roman poet Virgil (70-19 BC), added to the legend.

Homer's *Iliad* is essentially the story of Achilles set against events in the final year of the siege of Troy. His subject is not so much the Trojan War as a drama driven by strong personalities in which love competes with pride taken to excess, in a world of bloodshed and gore where even the gods, manipulating events from on high, reveal human emotions and weaknesses.

As with their counterparts in the oral and literary tradition, Greek artists felt free to be creative, re-interpreting the legend whilst drawing upon earlier depictions, rather than working from texts. The greatest paintings of the Sack of Troy by Polygnotos and Timanthes, from the fourth and fifth centuries BC, are lost, but the most prolific of Greek artists, the vase painters, have armed our imaginations (see Fig.2). Working in outline, within the shape of the vases, these decorative painters used attributes, subsidiary symbols and figures to illustrate favoured episodes from the Trojan War, confident that their viewers were familiar with the legend.

Sculptors similarly could be confined by the shape of a decorative commission. For example, the carved metopes on the north side of the Parthenon were devoted to the Sack of Troy. The *Medici Vase* (Uffizi, Florence) (Fig.3), a neo-Attic work of the first century AD, depicts Achilles, Agamemnon and Odysseus with Agamemnon's daughter Iphigenia. Sarcophagi, in which the richest Romans chose to be buried, carried reliefs that the imminent deceased considered appropriate (see Fig.4). One from around 230-40 AD in the Vatican depicts a crowded battle of Greeks against the Trojans' allies, the Amazons, in which the patron and his wife are portrayed respectively as Achilles and as Penthesilea, Queen of the Amazons.[2]

The most celebrated free-standing sculpture of a scene from the Trojan War, the *Laocoon* (Fig.5), is so frontal in its viewpoint as to be almost a relief in the round. In Virgil's *Aeneid* the Trojan priest is reported as denouncing the wooden horse as a deception, but after heaving a spear into its side a pair of sea-serpents crushes him and his sons. For centuries since its discovery in 1506 the *Laocoon* ranked alongside the *Apollo Belvedere* as the most famous and important Greek sculpture. Its origins are still uncertain, but its fame kept the Sack of Troy alive in artists' imaginations and, as an alternative to the graceful beauty of the *Apollo*, prompted debate about the expression of extreme emotion in art and poetry.

A group representing *Menelaos Carrying the Body of Patroclos* exists in three versions, the best known of which today stands in the Loggia dei Lanzi in Florence (Fig.6). Discovered not long before 1570, it was esteemed as an original Greek statue well into the nineteenth century but in fact is a replica of a Pergamene sculpture, carved between 240 and 230 BC. As a sculptural group conceived for multiple viewpoints, each carefully linked, it exerted a direct formal influence on sixteenth-century sculptors, most notably Michelangelo and Giovanni Bologna, who gave their groups a Biblical subject, *Samson and a Philistine*.

The two chief sources of the Troy legends for medieval artists were a supposed war diary kept by one Dictys Cretensis, of which a fourth-century AD Latin version survives, and a Latin account from the fifth century AD, *De excidio Troiae*, said to be originally by a Trojan priest named Dares Phrygius. These two forgeries, written in everyday Latin, seemed more accessible and reliable than Homer and were preferred by those favouring the Trojans as the true heroes. According to Virgil, Aeneas escaped from the Sack of Troy and his descendants founded the City of Rome.

The myth of Rome's descent from Troy still appealed during the Holy Roman Empire. Dictys and Dares were the

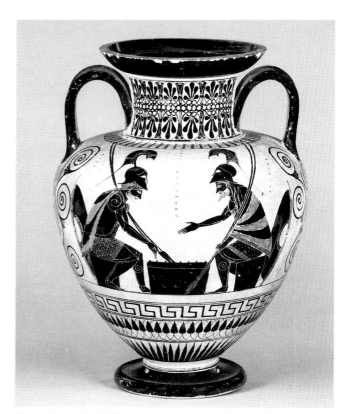

Fig.2 *Ajax and Achilles Playing a Game Resembling Backgammon*, Greek amphora, *c*.520 BC, British Museum.

Fig.3 The *Medici Vase*, marble, neo-Attic, second half of the first century AD, Uffizi, Florence (photo: Alinari).

basis for the verse romance *Roman de Troie*, written in French around 1160 by Benoît de Sainte-Maure. From this, and later sources, the story of the Trojan prince Troilus and his love for Cressida, set against the Trojan War, was developed in turn by Boccaccio, Chaucer and Shakespeare. Raoul Lefevre's *Collection of Trojan Histories* (1464) was translated by Caxton and in 1473-4 became the first book to be printed in English. In Spenser's *Faerie Queene* (1590, 1596) London is the 'New Troy' founded by Brutus the Trojan whose British subjects he originally named Brutuns. The legend's appeal in the medieval courts extended from literature to wall paintings, illuminated manuscripts, painted marriage chests and tapestries where the Greek and Roman heroes became Arthurian knights in an age of chivalry.

When parts of Homer were eventually translated from the original in the late fourteenth century, scholars studying Greek were disappointed by the lack of elegance, by the direct and graphic realism, but these were the 'Primitive' qualities which eighteenth-century Britain was to value so highly. None of these qualities are conveyed by the two Trojan subject paintings in London's National Gallery, *The Rape of Helen by Paris* (Fig.7), attributed to a follower of Fra Angelico (*c.*1450), and Pintoricchio's *Penelope With Her Suitors*, painted in 1509. More popular with the artists of the Renaissance and seventeenth century were the two amorous subjects involving gods and goddesses that predate Helen's departure: *Leda and the Swan* and *The Judgement of Paris*.

As with the literary tradition, visual images from the ancient world were re-cycled to strengthen some Biblical subjects. Deliberate allusion to the Troy legend was also possible for artists working within church patronage. For example, Raphael's *Fire in the Borgo* fresco in the Vatican would have been seen as a modern-day interpretation of the Sack of Troy with its foreground figure of Aeneas fleeing with his father Anchises on his back. Raphael's *Parnassus* (also in the Vatican *stanze*) shows the blind Homer dictating to Ennius, one of the inventors of shorthand and the author of a lost poem on the origins of Rome. Pride in the supposed ancestry of Romans led patrons to favour the tale of Aeneas over that of Achilles, and presumably lay behind, for example, Bernini's *Aeneas and Anchises* and the series of Aeneas paintings by Claude Lorrain.

The seventeenth century saw several English translations from Homer, but it was not until Alexander Pope's *Iliad* (1715-20) that Homer was to begin to have a real impact on British artists. The time was ripe, for Pope's interpretation coincided with the influence of translations of the Greek treatise *On the Sublime* ascribed to 'Longinus', with its emphasis on creative fire, on the writer's seriousness of thought and depth of emotion. The cult of the Sublime, valuing distress, terror, obscurity and solitude (in contrast to the qualities of smoothness and bright harmonious colours associated with the Beautiful) became more widespread after Edmund

Fig.4 *The Discovery of Achilles among the Daughters of Lycomedes*, Roman sarcophagus relief, *c.*200-250 AD, British Museum.

Burke's treatise *A Philosophical Enquiry Into the Origin of our Ideas of the Sublime and Beautiful* (1757). For artists, Homer's version of the siege of Troy became the essential text to fuel and articulate this alternative aesthetic.

Another emerging attitude that took Homer to the height of his popularity in eighteenth-century Britain was the taste for the Primitive, that led to a belief in the innate virtue of 'the noble savage'. According to Robert Wood's *Essay On the Original Genius and Writings of Homer* (1769), the poet was writing just when the Greeks were midway between emerging from their past barbarism and being spoilt by the cultivated qualities of civilisation. Homer seemed to evoke an unsophisticated, unaffected world where emotions could still be expressed directly. Homer's heroes might be impatient, deceitful, cruel, even childishly irritable and peevish to extremes, but they had a natural nobility, seriousness and a tendency to self-sacrifice, to commit heroic deeds and value honour to the death.

This duality in character and appeal could work either way and focused debate on the differences between the media in question. To the German theorist Winckelmann the antique sculpture of *Laocoon* illustrated the 'noble simplicity and calm grandeur' in attitude and expression that is typical of high classical Greek art, for he saw the Trojan priest suffering with dignity, his face not screaming in pain as the snake sinks its fangs into his writhing body and crushes his sons. Lessing, in his essay entitled *Laocoon, On the Limitations of Poetry and Painting* (1766) responded that whereas the sculptor showed restraint in the intensity of pained expression, his source and rival the poet, working in a less restrictive medium, could give full vent to the expression of emotion without loss of nobility: 'High as Homer exalts his heroes in other respects above human nature … in their feelings they are genuine human beings'.

The intellectual debate around Homer in the mid-eighteenth century was of particular interest to artists intent on shaking off any artisan status associated with the trades of interior decoration, topography and portraiture. The ambitions that led to the foundation of the Royal Academy in London in 1768 ensured that some artists would read the same texts as the 'men of letters', join in the debates and seek

Fig.5 *Laocoon*, marble, late Hellenistic, first century AD, Musei Vaticani, Rome (photo: Alinari).

Fig.6 *Menelaos Carrying the Body of Patroclos*, Roman, marble replica of a Pergamene group of *c*.240/230 BC, Loggia dei Lanzi, Florence (photo: Alinari).

to create independent works that were not subordinate to the taste and self-image of unsympathetic patrons. The first Academy president, Joshua Reynolds, used the annual prize-giving as an opportunity to inspire intellectual ambitions among British artists through a series of *Discourses* (from 1768 to 1790), in which repeated reference is made to the importance of reading Homer.

A few examples help to illustrate the status and appeal of Homer. In his third *Discourse* (1770) Reynolds quotes the classical writer Proclus on the sculptor of the Parthenon: 'Phidias, when he formed his Jupiter, did not copy any object ever presented to his sight; but contemplated only that image which he had conceived in his mind from Homer's description'.[3] He characterises the uplifting and ennobling benefits to be gained from reading Homer: 'The effect of the capital works of Michael Angelo [*sic*] perfectly corresponds to what Bouchardon said he felt from reading Homer; his whole frame appeared to himself to be enlarged, and all nature which surrounded him, diminished to atoms'.

Reynolds also cites the epic poet to illustrate the skilled use of contrast, the need for passages of quiet repose among bustle rather than being 'always on the stretch'. He recommends 'the practice of Homer, who, from the midst of battles and horrors, relieves and refreshes the mind of the reader, by

introducing some quiet rural image, or picture of familiar domestic life'.

By the time that Reynolds came to conclude his eleventh *Discourse* (1782) Homer is so basic to his audience's required reading that the president draws a parallel with a journey to Italy undertaken simply to copy pictures, measure statues and buildings. He warns that in the same way 'He that imitates the *Iliad* … is not imitating Homer. It is not by laying up in the memory the particular details of any of the great works of art, that any man becomes a great artist, if he stops without making himself master of the general principles on which these works are conducted.'

In his final *Discourse*, devoted to Michelangelo (1790), Reynolds feels that the essential quality in the works of Homer and Michelangelo that their imitators and interpreters missed was that of the Sublime, the sensation which 'so overpowers and takes such a possession of the whole mind, that no room is left for attention to minute criticism'.

The need to get back to the spirit of Homer, beyond the translations of poets and artists, demanded not only the promotion of the Sublime in art, but also, as mentioned earlier, of the Primitive. Alongside a growing desire to read Homer in the original lay the need for fresh visual sources. One solution was the art of Herculaneum and Pompeii, excavated from 1738 and 1748 respectively, particularly the two collections of painted vases formed by the British Envoy at the Court of Naples, Sir William Hamilton, and published in 1766/7 and in 1791/5. As flat, two-dimensional images in books independent of their decorative relation to vases, these designs offered not only a vocabulary of costume and compositions illustrating many recognisable scenes from the Trojan War but also a style that seemed suitably archaic and austere in approach. This was in marked contrast to mid-eighteenth-century Italian paintings of Trojan subjects, such as Gian Domenico Tiepolo's *Hall of the Iliad* in the Villa Valmara near Vicenza (*c*.1757) or his two *Trojan Horse* paintings now in the National Gallery, London (*c*.1760). (See Fig.8)

Interest in Homer and the Trojan War amongst British sculptors dates only from the last third of the eighteenth century. Initially the spread in admiration for Homer found expression in commissions for busts of the poet after the antique portrait traditionally identified as Homer. Alexander Pope bequeathed his own bust of Homer, believed to be by Bernini, to his protégé William Murray, first Earl of Mansfield, in 1744. In the great Library designed by Robert Adam for Mansfield at Kenwood, the overmantel portrait shows the Lord Chief Justice seated almost in conversation with this bust (Fig.10), which would have been the most prized work of art at Kenwood before the arrival of the Iveagh Bequest of paintings in 1928.

Casts and replicas of Homer's portrait were much in demand. When the portraitist John Smibert moved from England to America in 1728 he took with him possibly the first casts after the antique to reach the New World, namely a bust of Homer, a *Laocoon* and a *Venus de Medici*. John Cheere and Josiah Wedgwood both manufactured cast replicas of Homer's bust for use in libraries and Joseph Wilton carved marble copies of *Homer* (Kenwood) (Fig.9) and of the head of *Laocoon* (Victoria and Albert Museum). The other antique sculpture relating to the Trojan War to be favoured with reproduction was the *Medici Vase*, full size as garden ornaments and in miniature in bronze, alabaster and biscuit ware.

In the classically-inspired interiors of the great Palladian country houses of mid-eighteenth-century Britain, chimneypieces, overdoors and overmantels provided ample opportunity for sculptors to explore subjects from Greek and Roman literature, as too did the temples and other features of the British landscape garden. However, in this era British sculptors satisfied their patrons with marble translations of available engravings of classical sculptures, and these were not of Homeric subjects. The challenge of Greek sculpture lay in figures of ideal beauty such as Hercules, Apollo, Venus and Flora and the more ambitious sculptors sought comparison with the celebrated precedents through their own versions of the same subjects. It took the generation developing

Fig.7 Follower of Fra Angelico, *The Rape of Helen by Paris*, *c*.1450, panel, National Gallery, London.

Fig.8 Gian Domenico Tiepolo, *Procession of the Trojan Horse into Troy*, *c*.1760, oil on canvas, National Gallery, London.

in the 1770s to turn from their patrons' concern with the physical perfection of antique figures, from this burden of the past, to Homer's more human and heroic perception of the classical world.

Thomas Banks (1735/1805) is Britain's most admired sculptor of classical subjects and his sculptures more than answered Reynolds's aspirations (see Fig.11). Banks had been encouraged to pursue narrative subjects from Greek and Roman literature by premiums for sculpture awarded by the Society of Arts. The artists he met in Rome (1772/9), especially Fuseli and Sergel, shared his fascination with such themes, and their interpretations of scenes from the Trojan War have an intensity that belongs to the pre-Romantic world of their younger contemporary, William Blake. The range of emotion in Homer, and the oscillation between nobility and unseemly despair within the same characters, made the Trojan War an ideal source for artists keen to

Fig.9 Joseph Wilton, *Homer*, c.1760, marble bust, Iveagh Bequest, Kenwood.

Fig.10 David Martin, *William Murray, first Earl of Mansfield*, 1775, oil on canvas, Iveagh Bequest, Kenwood.

Fig.11 Thomas Banks, *Achilles Arming*, c.1776, terracotta, Victoria and Albert Museum.

explore the expressive limits of their medium, and to visualise the aesthetic qualities of the Sublime, rather than to re-create classical ideals of beauty.

The other great incentive to artists to study Homer, namely the discovery of visual source material in the vases from Herculaneum and Pompeii, was put to the greatest use by John Flaxman (1755-1826). Perhaps more familiar today through his designs for Wedgwood, Flaxman achieved international fame in his lifetime with his published books of outline images devoted to the writings of Homer, Aeschylus, Hesiod and Dante. To the portrait painter George Romney, Flaxman's outlines were so 'simple, grand and pure' that they seemed 'as if they had been made in the age when Homer wrote'.[4] His volumes on *The Iliad* and *The Odyssey* published in 1793 are austere in their minimal use of line but reveal a painstaking accuracy in the details of costume and furniture that came from studying Hamilton's vases and reading Homer in Greek (see Fig.12). Flaxman's *Shield of Achilles*, modelled in 1818, manufactured in silver gilt and sold to George IV in time for his coronation banquet in 1821, was a lifesize re-creation of Homer's detailed description in *The Iliad*, depicting both terrestrial and celestial scenes. Unlike the shield of Homer's imagination, it lacks only the colour that came from Hephaistos' use of a variety of metals and enamels.

This more archaeological approach to Homer had its parallels in the work of history painters[5] such as Gavin Hamilton and Benjamin West and may explain why, later in the nineteenth century, Homer, as with other classical

authors, became associated with 'academic' art. Flaxman's outlines illustrated innumerable paraphrases of the epic poems, books that became standard student prizes.

The great Greek Revival sculptors who dominated the first half of the nineteenth century produced Homeric subjects such as the statues of *Hector* by Canova and the Homeric reliefs by Thorwaldsen.[6] Subsequently the antique bard's appeal seems to have waned, presumably from over-familiarity, association with formal teaching, and the fact that artists no longer needed to use Homeric subjects to validate their professional status. Academic prizes continued to be offered for classical subjects, particularly the French Prix de Rome, but to the sculptors of Romanticism, few classical subjects appealed. Icarus, best known from Ovid's *Metamorphoses*, was one of the few to interest later nineteenth-century artists as he provided an archetype of ambitious youth. Of course, there was no shortage of *Sleeping Bacchantes* and *Bathing Nymphs*, the half-hearted titles adding respectability to the abundance of nudity. Instead of Achilles there was the more patriotic St George or modern military heroes almost queuing up to be commemorated in an age of Empire. The last great flourish, the colossal naked *Achilles* by Westmacott at Hyde Park Corner (1822), was considered an appropriate tribute to the Duke of Wellington during his lifetime from the women of Britain.

Homer is central in the reliefs on the Albert Memorial (1863-72) with Dante and Shakespeare reclining at his feet, but there are no great Homeric compositions by the leading

British sculptors of the Victorian age. Among the painters, Turner explored Virgil's tale of Aeneas, and the face of Helen fascinated the Pre-Raphaelite era with its renewed interest in ideal beauty, the *femme fatale* and the 'fallen woman' (see Fig.13). William Morris translated Homer and Virgil and composed poems on the fall of Troy. The medieval interpretation of Homer's heroes as Arthurian knights also enjoyed a brief revival in the paintings of Burne-Jones, possibly encouraged by the discovery of the remains of Troy by Heinrich Schliemann in 1873.

For most of the twentieth century, historical and literary subjects seem to have been of interest to only a handful of sculptors. Epstein and Moore sought out alternative traditions afresh, in African, Pacific and pre-Colombian sculpture. Surrealism encouraged the use of suggestion and random association in the viewer's mind, and some link with the figurative tradition continued in the expressionist sculpture of the 1950s and 1960s produced by the generation of Butler, Paolozzi and Frink. But a greater departure from sculpture's 'fine art' legacy of classical subjects came with the emphasis on the 'pure' sculptural values of mass, void, tension and materials as ends in themselves. Free from making any references, the autonomous abstract work of art might be enjoyed like music and dance, primarily as a moving composition.

Hitherto, Anthony Caro's contribution to sculpture has been valued primarily in terms of abstract qualities. After training as an engineer, he worked as Henry Moore's assistant until, in 1953, he began to produce sculptures of bulky human figures inspired by the random shapes formed by dropping and hitting soft clay. A rough, unfinished appearance resulted after casting, which retained the sense of the artist at work, of the process of creation that now seems akin to the 'truth to materials' and 'direct carving' ethics associated with Moore and Hepworth. Caro retained this fascination with the innate qualities of materials and the value of leaving evidence of the creative process in the finished work when, around 1959-60, he left clay, plaster and the figurative tradition for the medium he made his own, painted steel.

Appreciation of Caro's sculptures has dwelt on his strength as a composer, on the dances and surprises through which his works lead the viewer's wandering gaze, on the relationship between the poise and proportions of the sculpture and of the viewer. But there is another love, which reminds us that there has always been another dimension to his work, namely Caro's poetical use of titles, for mere numbers do not seem to satisfy. His interest in Greek poetry comes as less of a surprise when one recognises the associations and animation he brings to sculpture through the quiet, apposite (and occasionally eccentric and humorous) addition of evocative names. Some of the most memorable are: *Early One Morning*, *Night Movements*, *Barcelona Ballad*, *Month of May*, *Ordnance*, *Orangerie*, *Hopscotch*, *Xanadu*, *Red Splash* and *Elephant Palace*.

Fig.12 *Diomed Casting his Spear against Mars*, plate 12 from the *Iliad* illustrations by John Flaxman, 1793.

This psychological, rather than purely optical concern might appear inconsistent with the deliberate avoidance of reference to other forms in his sculpture. For example, when first using I-beams in the 1960s Caro preferred to explore horizontal compositions rather than incur allusion to the human figure which almost any upright might suggest to a public accustomed to modern sculpture. Spread over forty years, his career could be divided into the exploration of a series of formal themes, fulfilling his belief that 'sculpture needs to be reinvented again and again', with the restless adventurous artist forever experimenting, seeking 'a new vocabulary for sculpture'. But linking the abstract series, the floor pieces, table pieces, architectural compositions, there is this poetic use of titles that enriches our emotional response and implies a creative mind reluctant to lose the greater dimension that comes through subject-matter.

In 1985 Anthony Caro visited Greece for the first time and was inspired by the combination of sculpture and architecture he saw at Olympia and on the Acropolis, by the 'sensual rolling forms and figures contained and even forced into strict architectural shapes'. *After Olympia* (1987), inspired by the group of nearly twenty battling Lapiths and Centaurs on the west pediment on the temple of Zeus at Olympia, is his largest sculpture and an overt declaration of Caro's recognition of the continuity, the shared interest, between abstract sculpture and the masterpieces of the past. It is as if a career of 'reinventing' sculpture has revealed the common ground that unites sculptors across the centuries. The inclusion of *After Olympia* in an exhibition in the second-century Trajan Markets overlooking the Forum in Rome in 1992 underlines this sense of shared ambitions. It also reminds us, as with Caro's use of titles, that his choice of settings for his sculptures (particularly in the photographs he selects to illustrate his œuvre) is not confined to the neutral white gallery spaces usually associated with abstract sculpture.

Caro has long been seeking to create 'a kind of War and Peace sculpture', a complex multi-figure composition. Seen as one group rather than as a collection of nearly forty individual sculptures, *The Trojan War* goes beyond *After Olympia* in fulfilling this ambition. The immediate origins of the group

Fig.13 Dante Gabriel Rossetti, *Helen of Troy*, 1863, oil on canvas, Hamburger Kunsthalle.

elevates a sculpture from the space in which the viewer stands, may seem a contradiction of one of Caro's characteristic achievements. But back in his London studio the creative process took off, as each 'pedestal' became an integral part of these volumetric sculptures, some supporting intricate steel compositions appropriate to the emerging identities. The gradual development of the ceramics with wood and steel until they became upright constructions recalls the collage sculptures of Picasso and Julio Gonzalez of the 1930s, with their similar allusion to anatomy. Echoes of Surrealism and African sculpture may also be heard. The human scale of the finished compositions reflects the intensity of the sculptor working alone indoors, the attention to detail creating a sense of secrecy, and the effect of hidden clues, attributes and surprises within the sculptures. The rugged materials and rough finish that come from preferring to leave evidence of the creative process add to the sense of confronting unearthed artefacts. It is almost as though the artist has turned archaeologist and excavated the battlefield beneath the walls of Troy.

Caro's return to using solid volume and conscious allusion to the human figure for the first time since the 1950s reflects a confidence in the continuing relevance of sculpture's most enduring themes. The Primitive and Sublime qualities of *The Trojan War* bind the group to Homer and to a traditional concern among artists. This is not the 'academic' tradition of seeking out ideal beauty by copying plaster casts after the antique. Rather, it is the belief in the need to reach back into the origins of art, to find a language to explore and express the full range of human emotion and outlook, in a way so powerful that the viewer cannot ignore it.

lay in a visit in April 1993 to Grasse on the Côte d'Azure north of Nice to the studio of Hans Spinner, a ceramicist who has worked with European painters, including Miró. Caro had experimented in clay twice before in his career, in the 1950s (as mentioned earlier) and in 1975 when an invitation to join a workshop of leading artists at Syracuse University, New York, resulted in sculptures that took the customary vessel forms of ceramic ware, sliced them and then combined them like still-lives by Cézanne or Braque. But this was something completely new to Caro — rather than the fifteen per cent grog normally added, Spinner's clay was sixty per cent grog, thereby avoiding the technical necessity of hollowing out the model before firing and so encouraging the sculptor to stick with solid volume. Consequently the finished stoneware retained the rugged effects from the moment at which the sculptor finally stepped back. They also emerged from the kiln with an added drama due to the tonal variations caused by fire.

'I worked very loosely, intuitively', Caro says. 'I allowed the clay and the lumps, what Hans calls "the breads" to take me. We pushed and beat things into the clay until an image began to emerge.' It was after placing the 'head' now known as *Homer* on a makeshift pedestal that 'they began to speak, they became gods and heroes'.

This return to the pedestal, the element that essentially

Notes

1. For example, a significant exception is the legend of the Minotaur which inspired etchings by Picasso and sculptures by Michael Ayrton. De Chirico painted a *Hector and Andromache* series (1916-24). In recent years British sculptors such as Ian Hamilton Finlay and Stephen Cox have incorporated more fundamental classical references into their work.

2. Illustrated in Susan Woodford *The Trojan War in Ancient Art* (London, 1993) p.91. For a more extensive illustration of the Trojan War, particularly in medieval art, see Margaret R. Scherer *The Legends of Troy in Art and Literature* (New York and London, 1963).

3. Sir Joshua Reynolds *Discourses on Art*, ed. Robert R. Wark (New Haven and London, 1975) *passim*.

4. Romney quoted in Robert Rosenblum *Transformations in Late Eighteenth Century Art* (Princeton, 1974) p.172.

5. For comparisons of the most popular *Iliad* subjects see: D. Wiebenson 'Subjects from Homer's Iliad in Neoclassical Art', *Art Bulletin*, 46, 1964, pp.23-37.

6. See, for example, the versions of the first relief Thorwaldsen carved in Rome in 1803, *Briseis Led Away from Achilles by the Heralds of Agamemnon*, at Woburn Abbey and Chatsworth.

The Trojan War
John Spurling

The History

The ancient city of Troy, also known as Ilion, stood on a low hill near the mouth of the Dardanelles on the eastern side of the Aegean Sea. Excavations have disclosed nine layers of ruins on the site. The seventh layer up – dating from about 1230 BC – may once have been the city destroyed in the legendary Trojan War. Its story was told some 500 years afterwards by the Greek singer-poet Homer in *The Iliad* and *The Odyssey*, but the poems were not written down until a century later – about 650 BC – when they had already become, for all the Greeks living around the Aegean, the central fount of their history, myth, religion and race-consciousness. Admired, imitated and plundered by the writers and artists of ancient Rome as well as Greece, the poems have been, with the Bible, the prime sources of characters, stories and material for European art, literature and music over the past 600 years.

'Greeks' and 'Greece' are terms used by the ancient Romans. The inhabitants called their country 'Hellas' and themselves 'Hellenes', but not until after Homer's time. He usually calls them 'Achaians' (pronounced *Akee'ans* in English).

The Story

Paris, second son of King Priam of Troy, is chosen by the Olympian gods to judge which of three powerful goddesses – Hera, Athene or Aphrodite – is the most beautiful. Each goddess offers him a bribe, but Aphrodite's – the love of the most beautiful woman on earth – is the one he prefers. Aphrodite, therefore, wins the contest and Paris crosses the sea to Greece to collect his reward. There he is entertained by the King of Sparta, Menelaos, with whose wife Helen he falls in love. Together they run away to Troy.

Menelaos and his brother Agamemnon gather ships and men from all the various cities and districts of Greece and land near Troy. The Trojans meanwhile summon help from their neighbours and a ten-year war begins. It is not so much a siege as a constant series of hand-to-hand battles led by the principal heroes, with intermittent interference by the gods, on the plain between Troy and the Greek camp on the shore.

In the tenth year of inconclusive fighting – though the gods know that the Trojans will lose in the end – the Greeks suffer a serious setback. Their greatest champion, Achilles, quarrels violently with Agamemnon, the commander-in-chief, over a captured slave-girl and refuses to take any further part in the war. As if this were not bad enough, Achilles' immortal mother Thetis persuades Zeus, King of the gods, to allow the Trojans to make such headway in Achilles' absence that Agamemnon will be forced to give in to him. Zeus orders the other gods to stop helping either side and the Trojans, led by their champion Hector, begin to drive the Greeks back on their ships. The Greeks throw up a rampart to protect their camp, but the Trojans break through it and start to burn the ships.

Now even Achilles, who has rejected all Agamemnon's overtures and is still sulking in his tent, grows alarmed. He lends his own armour, his chariot and troops to his friend Patroclos, who turns the tide of battle and drives the Trojans back to the walls of their city. But there Patroclos is killed by Hector and stripped of his borrowed armour. This disaster brings Achilles himself back into the battle, equipped with magnificent new arms and armour – his mother Thetis has had them made for him overnight by the craftsman-god Hephaistos. Achilles drives the Trojans inside their city and, after pursuing Hector three times round the walls, kills him, strips him and drags the body ignominiously away behind his chariot.

The Iliad ends with Hector's funeral, after his corpse has been begged from Achilles by King Priam. The rest of the story is told in *The Odyssey* and later literature. Achilles dies from an arrow shot by Paris, but Troy is finally captured when the Greeks pretend to give up and sail away, leaving behind on the shore a huge wooden horse. The triumphant Trojans, believing it to be some offering to the gods, drag it inside the city and retire to sleep. Then the armed Greeks hidden inside the belly of the horse emerge, open the gates of Troy to their secretly returned army outside, and sack the city.

Not all the Greeks live happily ever after. Agamemnon is murdered by his unfaithful wife Clytemnestra as soon as he gets home to Mycenae; Odysseus takes ten years to return to his faithful wife Penelope in Ithaca and all his men die on the way. The beautiful Helen, however, settles down again as Menelaos' queen in Sparta. After all, as she points out, her love-affair with Paris and the ensuing Trojan War were really Aphrodite's doing.

THE POET
Homer   Ομηρος

A poet about whom nothing is known for certain. He is thought to have lived on the east coast of the Aegean (now Anatolia) in about 750-700 BC and to have composed both *The Iliad* and *The Odyssey*. Homer was traditionally said to be blind and to have portrayed himself in *The Odyssey* as the poet/singer Demodocos:

> The steward came in, escorting a distinguished singer much favoured by the muse, though she had given him both good and bad fortune, making his songs sweet but depriving him of his sight. Pontonoos, the steward, set a silver-studded chair for him against a large pillar at the centre of the feast and hung his clear-toned lyre from a nail above his head, showing him where to find it with his hands . . . When they had all had enough to eat and drink, the singer's muse moved him to sing of the exploits of heroes . . .
> *Odyssey* VIII 62-73

Homer 1993/4
Ceramic and steel
51 × 14 × 14 in (130 × 36 × 36 cm)

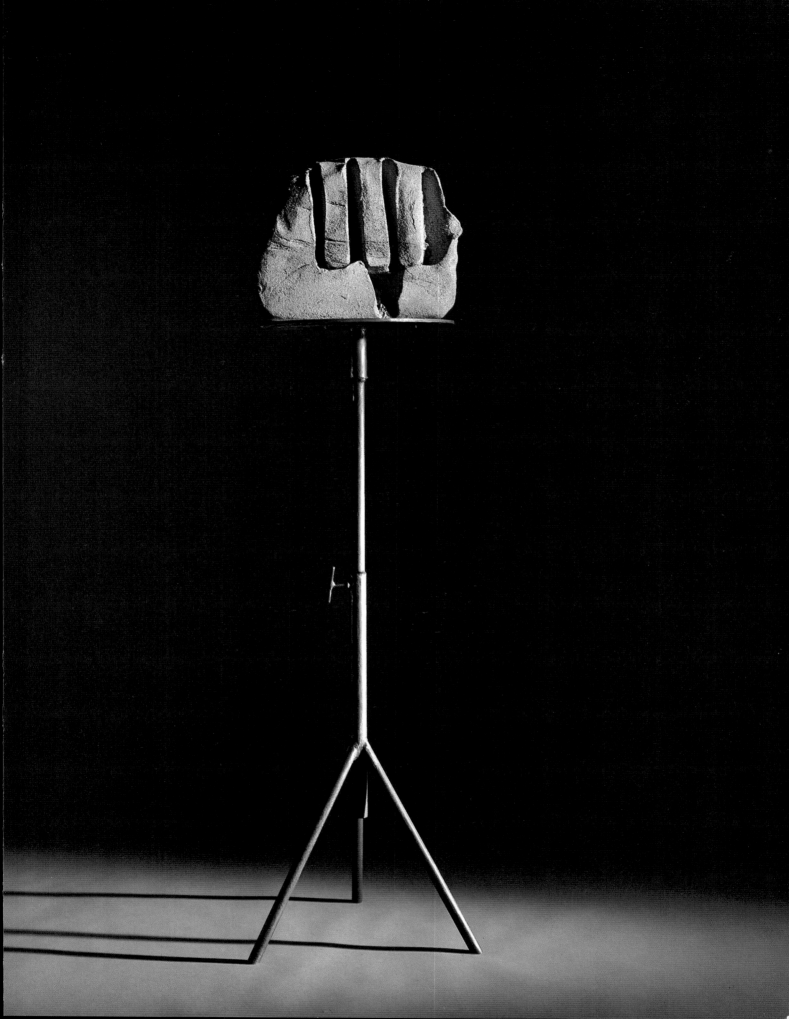

THE OLYMPIAN GODS
Zeus   Ζευς

The patriarch of the Olympian gods, who are mostly his
relations. He takes no direct part in the Trojan War on the ground,
but observes and manipulates events.

> 'I find mortal men very touching. But I shall stay here on
> Mount Olympos, sitting in a sheltered spot, and shall be
> satisfied with watching. The rest of you can go down
> among the Trojans and Achaians and give help to
> whichever side you like.'
> *Iliad* xx 21 ⁄ 5

Zeus 1993/4
Ceramic and steel
79 × 24 × 17 in (179 × 61 × 43 cm)

3

THE OLYMPIAN GODS
Ares   Αρης

God of war, son of Zeus and Hera, but disliked by almost everyone, including his parents. He is violent, terrifying and unreliable. At one point, while helping the Trojans, he is wounded by Athene:

> Bronze-armoured Ares roared as loud as nine or ten thousand warriors all roaring together in the middle of a battle fought in the name of himself, the god of war. So appalling was Ares' roaring, the noise of the insatiable god of war, that terror gripped Achaians and Trojans alike.
> *Iliad* v 859-63

Ares (War) 1993/4
Ceramic and painted steel
54 × 22½ × 21 in (137 × 57 × 53.5 cm)

4

THE OLYMPIAN GODS
Hera Ηρη

Wife and sister of Zeus, vehemently pro-Achaian, as also is Athene, because the Trojan prince Paris tactlessly and disastrously awarded the prize for beauty to the love goddess Aphrodite rather than to either of them. Hera is less powerful than her husband/brother, but she is never a docile wife. At one point, when the battle is going badly for the Achaians and Zeus has strictly forbidden the gods to intervene, Hera resorts to sex and the collaboration of the minor deity Hypnos (Sleep) to outwit him:

> So, overcome by sleep and love-making, the father dozed quietly on the peak of Mount Gargaron, holding his wife in his arms; meanwhile Hypnos ran to the Achaian ships with a message for the god of seas and earthquakes: 'Now, Poseidon, you have a short time in which to give all the help and glory you like to the Achaians. Zeus is asleep. Hera enticed him into lying down and making love and I've put him into a mild coma.'
> *Iliad* XIV 352-60

Hera 1993/4
Ceramic and steel
$57\frac{1}{2} \times 19 \times 20$ in (146 × 49 × 51 cm)

5

THE OLYMPIAN GODS
Athene   Αθηναιη

Goddess of wisdom and war, born from the head of Zeus.
For the same reason as Hera, Athene is pro-Achaian:

> The Achaian leaders hurried to gather their forces and
> with them went grey-eyed Athene, bearing the aegis — the
> magnificent and indestructible storm-cloud shield, with its
> hundred golden tassels, each woven separately, each worth
> a hundred cattle. Dazzling bright she flew through the
> Achaian ranks and pressed them forward; in every heart
> she roused the will to fight and struggle on without stop-
> ping; at that moment war seemed sweeter to them than
> returning in the hollow ships to the homes and countries
> they loved.
> *Iliad* II 445-54

Athene 1993/4
Ceramic and steel
60 × 18 × 20 in (152 × 46 × 51 cm)

6

THE OLYMPIAN GODS
Aphrodite   Αφροδιτη

Goddess of love, daughter of Zeus, but not of Hera. The Trojan prince Paris awarded her the prize for beauty in competition with Hera and Athene; in return Aphrodite gave Paris what she had promised him in advance – the love of the most beautiful woman in the world. This happened to be the Greek (Achaian) Helen, already married to Menelaos, King of Sparta, and the Trojan War was the consequence of Helen absconding with Paris to Troy. Aphrodite remains loyally pro-Trojan, but being generous, compliant and somewhat innocent by nature is easily deceived by Hera into lending her a love-charm for devious anti-Trojan purposes:

> Aphrodite, who loves smiles . . . unfastened from her breast the embroidered band; every kind of seduction was woven into it: friendship, desire and sweet conversation, which infatuates even the most sensible people.
> *Iliad* XIV 211-17

Aphrodite 1993/4
Ceramic and steel
70½ × 15 × 15 in (179 × 38 × 38 cm)

7

THE OLYMPIAN GODS
Apollo   Απολλων

God of light, he is pro‑Trojan and very active on their behalf. At one point he finds the Trojan hero Aeneas dispirited by the constant superiority of the Achaian champion Achilles:

'Just aim your hard bronze straight and don't let him put you down with threats and sneers!'
With these words Apollo breathed high courage into this leader of men and he pushed into the front rank of warriors, his bronze arms flashing.
Iliad XX 108‑11

Apollo 1993/4
Ceramic and steel
61 × 32 × 17½ in (155 × 81 × 44.5 cm)

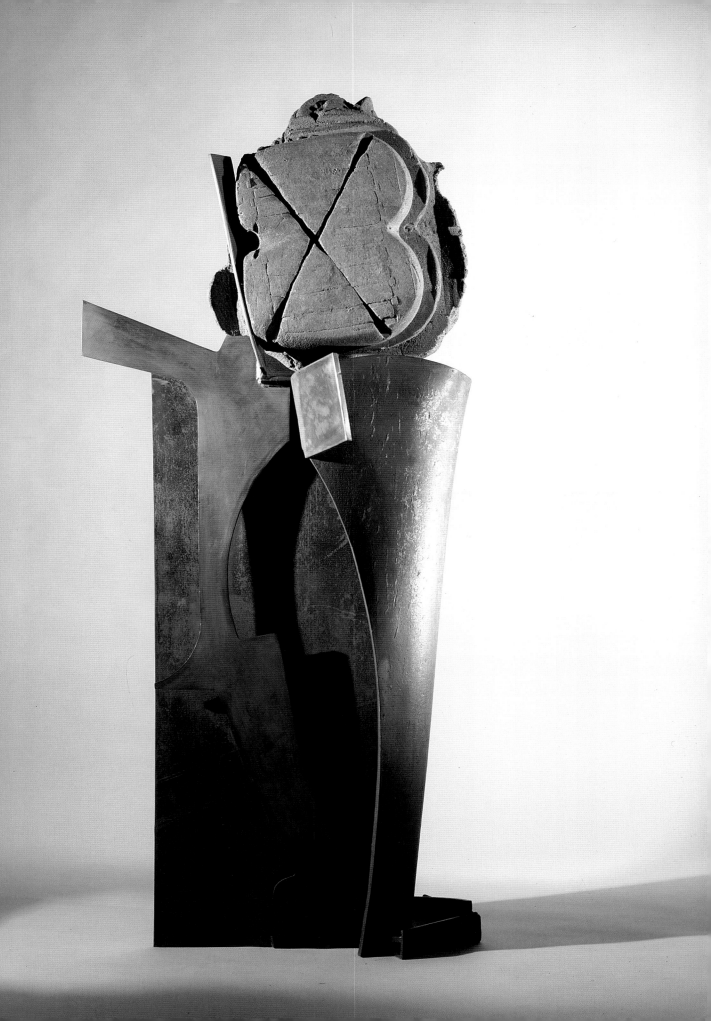

8

THE OLYMPIAN GODS
Poseidon　　　　　　　　　Ποσειδαων

The sea-god, younger brother of Zeus. He is generally pro-
Achaian because he helped build the walls of Troy for the city's
founder and was not given the agreed reward. But he is a particularly
touchy god and becomes angry with the Achaians too when they build
a rampart on the sea-shore to protect their ships against the Trojans,
without making the appropriate sacrifice to him. Zeus tells him sharply
not to worry:

'For Heaven's sake, what are you saying? You are the god
of earthquakes, your authority is vast! This idea might
alarm some other god with less physical power or less force
of will than you; but your glory extends as far as the light
of dawn. When the long-haired Achaians sail home to
their own country, pull down the rampart, sweep the whole
thing into the sea and cover the long beach with sand!'
Iliad VII 455-62

Poseidon 1993/4
Ceramic and steel
$40\frac{1}{2} \times 38\frac{1}{2} \times 23\frac{1}{2}$ in (102.5 × 98 × 58 cm)

9

THE OLYMPIAN GODS
Hermes   Ερμης

Intermediary between gods and men. Towards the end
of *The Iliad* when Achilles has killed the Trojan hero Hector and
dragged his corpse to the Achaian camp, Hector's father Priam,
King of Troy, sets out to beg his son's body for burial:

> Zeus pitied the old man and immediately spoke to his dear
> son Hermes: 'You enjoy making friends with mortals,
> Hermes, and you listen to anyone who attracts you. Go
> quickly and guide Priam to the Achaian ships, making
> sure that no one sees him and that he reaches Achilles
> without any of the other Achaians knowing!' The swift,
> shining courier . . . tied on his feet the beautiful, golden,
> gods' sandals which would carry him over water or any
> stretch of land as quickly as a gust of wind; and he picked
> up the magic wand with which he could charm any man's
> eyes asleep, or wake anyone already sleeping; and flew
> straight to Troy.
> *Iliad* XXIV 332⁄46

Hermes 1993/4
Ceramic and steel
47 × 22 × 12 in (119.5 × 56 × 30 cm)

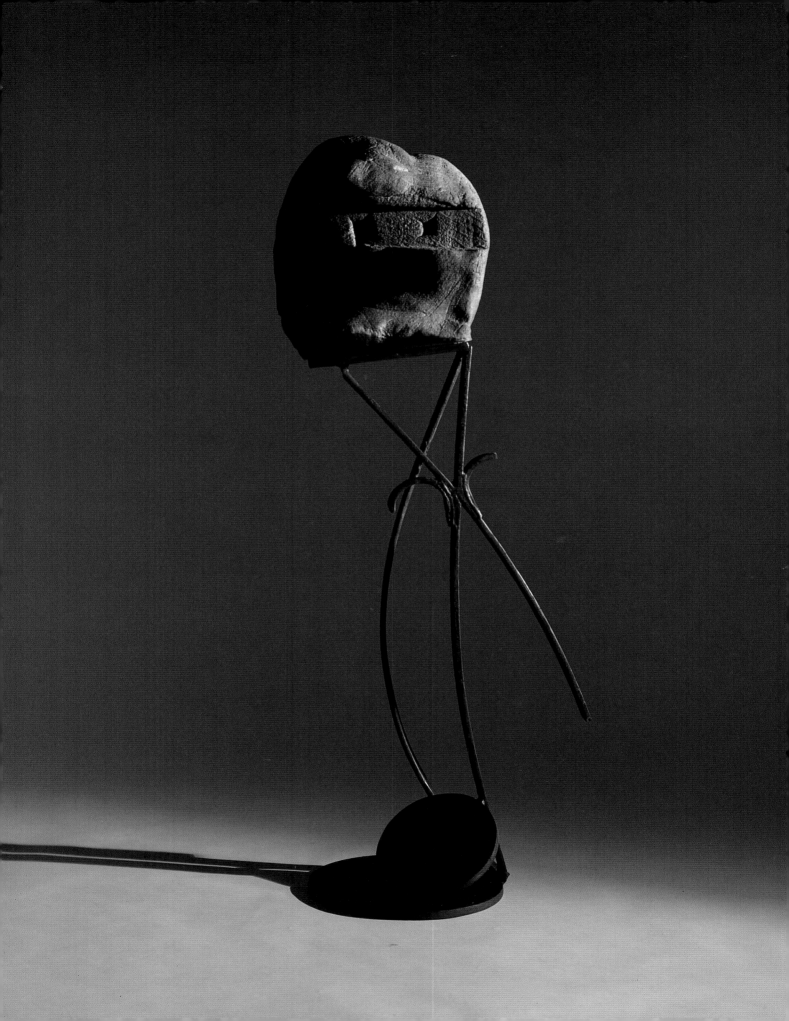

THE OLYMPIAN GODS
Hephaistos   Ηφαιστος

The god of fire, crafts and arts. Achilles' mother, Thetis,
visits Hephaistos to ask him to make her son a new set of arms and
armour. She is received in an adjoining room by Hephaistos' wife,
while the lame welder/fitter makes himself presentable:

> He straightened up from the anvil, breathing heavily, a
> limping giant; but his thin legs moved rapidly. He fetched
> the bellows away from the fire, collected all the tools he had
> been using and put them together in a silver chest; with
> a sponge he wiped both sides of his face and both hands,
> his strong neck and hairy chest; then he put on a sleeveless
> tunic, picked up a good walking/stick and went limping
> through the door.
> *Iliad* XVIII 410/17

Hephaistos 1993/4
Ceramic and steel
53 × 30½ × 12½ in (140 × 77.5 × 32 cm)

THE OLDER GODS
Helios (Sun)   Ηλιος

Homer frequently juxtaposes, without explicit comment, the sun's light – and its associated sense of well-being and optimism – with the action on the ground, for instance the collection of the dead during a truce:

> The sun was just striking the fields with light as he rose
> out of deep-running Ocean and climbed the sky; and the
> two parties met. It was difficult to recognise any particular
> man; cleaning the blood from their wounds with water,
> weeping warm tears, they loaded them on carts.
> *Iliad* VII 421-6

On another day:

> While it was early and the day still fresh the missiles kept
> raining down from both sides and warriors kept falling.
> But as the Sun moved round to the middle of the sky, the
> father balanced his golden scales and put in them two
> symbols of fate, weights for bitter death, one for the horse-
> taming Trojans and one for the bronze-armoured
> Achaians; grasping the scales in the middle he held them
> up. The destiny of the Achaians sank.
> *Iliad* VIII 66-72

Helios (Sun) 1993/4
Ceramic and ash wood
34 × 24 × 16 in (86.5 × 61 × 41 cm)

THE OLDER GODS
Eos (Dawn)   Ηως

Now Dawn in her saffron cloak spread light over
all the earth.
Iliad VIII 1

Eos (Dawn) 1993/4
Ceramic and steel
30 × 42 × 29 in (76 × 107 × 74 cm)

THE OLDER GODS
Nux (Night)   Νυξ

Night, the empress of gods and men . . .
Iliad XIV 259

Nux (Night) 1993/4
Ceramic and steel
57 × 30½ × 24 in (145 × 77.5 × 61 cm)

THE OLDER GODS
Scamander   Σκαμανδρος

River rising on Mount Ida and flowing past Troy. The river-god becomes infuriated when the Achaian champion Achilles pursues a rout of Trojans into the water and dams the normally gentle, clear stream with slaughtered corpses:

The great spearman Achilles leaped from the overhanging bank and landed in the middle of the river, which gathered all its waters into an angry spate and surged towards him in a huge wave, carrying along many of the bodies of Achilles' victims which had settled in heaps on the bed
. . .

Achilles sprang out of the swirling current and ran with all his speed over the plain; he was afraid. But the powerful god did not let him go; he poured after him in a black boiling flood . . .

Achilles doubled back the length of a spear-throw, swooping like a black hunting eagle, the strongest and swiftest of all birds, while the bronze armour on his breast rattled grimly. Then on he went, desperately racing from under the wave, but the torrent rolled on behind him, rumbling and roaring.

Iliad XXI 233-56

Scamander 1993/4
Ceramic and steel
$45\frac{1}{2} \times 28 \times 21$ in ($116 \times 71 \times 53$ cm)

THE OLDER GODS
Hypnos (Sleep)   Ὕπνος

. . . Sleep, the brother of Death.
Iliad XIV 231

Hypnos (Sleep) 1993/4
Ceramic, jarrah wood and steel
$58\frac{1}{2} \times 21 \times 18$ in ($149 \times 53.5 \times 46$ cm)

THE OLDER GODS
Thanatos (Death) Θανατος

Death is personified in *The Iliad* only as an adjunct to
Sleep. Demanding the death of the Trojan hero Sarpedon, Hera says:

> 'As soon as his life and soul have left him, send Death and
> painless Sleep to bear him to his people in the pleasant land
> of Lycia.'
> *Iliad* XVI 453·4

Thanatos (Death) 1993/4
Ceramic, pine wood and jarrah wood
$56\frac{1}{2} \times 22 \times 11\frac{1}{2}$ in ($143.5 \times 66 \times 29.5$ cm)

17

THE ACHAIANS
The Achaians
Αχαιοι

The general name by which Homer usually refers to the thirty or so different tribes from all over Greece who crossed the sea in more than a thousand ships to attack Troy.

All the many tribes of Achaians poured out from their ships and huts onto the plain of Scamander and the earth throbbed grimly under the tread of men and horses. They stood in the flowery meadows beside the River Scamander – innumerable as leaves and flowers in their seasons. Like many species of flies buzzing and swarming round a cow-shed in spring when milk is splashing into jugs, the long-haired Achaians took up position against the Trojans, ready to destroy them.

Iliad II 464-73

The Achaians 1993/4
Ceramic and steel
$91\frac{1}{2} \times 66\frac{1}{2} \times 36\frac{1}{2}$ in (232.5 × 169 × 93 cm)

18

THE ACHAIANS
Agamemnon Αγαμεμνων

King of Mycenae and the most powerful Achaian ruler, he organised the Achaian expedition against Troy on behalf of his brother, Menelaos. Agamemnon is in overall command of the Achaians, but he is arrogant, domineering and easily discouraged – too seldom in command of himself. He gives disastrous offence to Achilles and, when he finally gets home at the end of the war, is brutally murdered by his wife Clytemnestra. Still, he cuts a fine figure as the Achaians muster for battle:

> ... and chief of them all, Agamemnon, his eyes and his head like Zeus', king of thunder, his waist like the god of war's, his chest like the sea-god Poseidon's. As a bull is conspicuous in a herd of cattle, as he can be picked out from a mass of cows, so Zeus this day picked Agamemnon out of the crowd and made him conspicuous among the heroes.

Iliad II 477-83

Agamemnon 1993/4
Ceramic, jarrah wood and steel
70 × 25 × 12½ in (178 × 63.5 × 32 cm)

19

THE ACHAIANS
Menelaos   Μενελαος

The red-haired King of Sparta, husband of the beautiful
Helen, is a spirited and sympathetic young hero, but rash. When
Achilles is sulking in his tent, Hector challenges any of the other
Achaians to meet him in single combat. There is an uneasy silence
in the Achaian ranks, finally broken by Menelaos:

> 'Are you really only good at boasting? Are you Achaian
> women, not Achaian men? This will be the most appal-
> ling disgrace, if not a single one of the Achaians will take
> on Hector. I wish you would all dissolve into the dust and
> water you came from, sitting there, every one of you, like
> cowards, like scum! Well, *I* will put on my armour for
> him. After all, the reins of victory are held from above, by
> the immortal gods.'

> With these words he fastened on his splendid armour.
> And now, Menelaos, it looked as if your life's end would
> be in the hands of Hector, since he was much the greater
> warrior, if the Achaian leaders had not leapt up and held
> you back . . .

Iliad VII 96-106

Menelaos 1993/4
Ceramic, steel and jarrah wood
$66\frac{1}{2} \times 19 \times 13\frac{1}{2}$ in (169 × 49 × 34 cm)

20

THE ACHAIANS
Patroclos   Πατροκλος

Inseparable friend of his cousin Achilles, with whom he
was brought up and educated. Together with Achilles, Patroclos
withdraws from the fighting, but when the Trojans look like winning,
disguises himself in Achilles' armour and drives them back, until he
is killed by Hector. In a fury of revenge Achilles slaughters innumerable Trojans, including Hector, but reserves twelve Trojan prisoners
for Patroclos' funeral:

They made a pyre one hundred feet long and wide and,
grieving deeply, laid the body on top. In front of the pyre
they flayed and prepared a large number of sheep and curly-
horned cattle; from these the noble Achilles took the fat
and covered the corpse with it from head to foot, then
heaped the carcases all round. He added two-handled jars
of honey and ointment, leaning them against the bier; then,
crying aloud with anguish, quickly threw four horses with
high-arching necks onto the pyre. Of the nine hounds fed
from their master's table he cut the throats of two and threw
them on the pyre; and killed with his sword the twelve
brave sons of noble Trojans – an ugly, premeditated deed.
Then he started the inexorable fire that would consume
it all.
Iliad XXIII 164-77

The Body of Patroclos 1993/4
Ceramic, oak wood and steel
60 × 55 × 23 in (152.5 × 140 × 59 cm)

21

THE ACHAIANS
Achilles   Αχιλευς

Son of a Thessalian king and the sea-goddess Thetis,
Achilles is the hero of heroes and the most complex character in *The
Iliad*: proud, generous, intelligent, sensitive and often gloomy – he
knows he is doomed to die young. During much of the story, however,
he is hardly himself: first angry and unemployed, deprived of his
favourite slave-girl and with his weapons and armour hung up
uselessly in his tent; then, after the death of his friend Patroclos, berserk
with grief. His mother finds him embracing the corpse and gives him
the new arms and armour specially made for him by Hephaistos:

> When Achilles saw them he was even more possessed with
> rage and his eyes glittered savagely under the lids like
> flames; then he took the god's magnificent gifts in his hands
> and was delighted. But when his pleasure in looking at the
> workmanship was satisfied, he spoke urgently to his
> mother:
> 'Mother, the arms the god has given are fit for gods – things
> no man could make – and now I will certainly put them
> on and prepare to fight. But I am terribly afraid that mean-
> while flies will get into brave Patroclos through the wounds
> made by the bronze spears and breed maggots and dis-
> honour his body. Its life has been destroyed, so all the flesh
> will rot.'
> *Iliad* XIX 15-27

Achilles 1993/4
Ceramic and steel
66 × 37 × 21 in (168 × 94 × 53.5 cm)

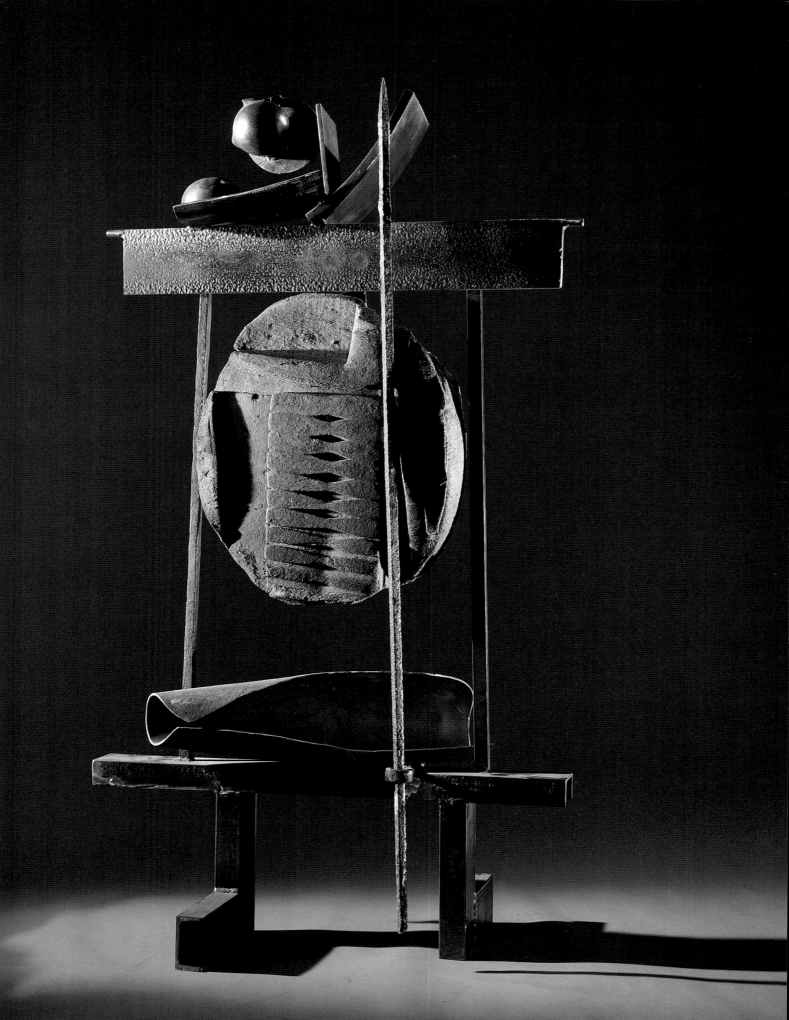

22

THE ACHAIANS
The Chariot of Achilles   Αρμα Αχιλης

Achilles goes out to avenge Patroclos:

> Automedon and Alkimos were busy yoking the horses,
> putting fine collars round them and bits in their jaws and
> taking the reins back to the chariot. Automedon grasped
> the gleaming whip attached to the chariot and jumped up
> on the platform. Behind him mounted Achilles, his helmet
> and armour shining with the brilliance of the sun.
> *Iliad* XIX 392/8

The Chariot of Achilles 1993/4
Ceramic, concrete, wood and steel
32 × 46 × 56½ (81.5 × 117 × 143.5 cm)

23

THE ACHAIANS
Xanthos   Ξανθος

One of the two immortal horses which draw Achilles'
chariot. The name Xanthos refers to its colour: sorrel or chestnut.
After Patroclos has ridden into battle in the chariot and been killed
by Hector, the driver cannot make the horses turn back to the safety
of the camp:

> Like a gravestone marking the tomb of a dead man or
> woman, they stood there, with the beautiful chariot, com-
> pletely motionless, their heads bent down to the ground.
> Hot tears dropped from their eyes into the dust as they wept
> with longing for their charioteer. Their long manes flowing
> down on either side of the pads under the yoke were
> covered in dirt. Zeus saw them mourning and pitied them;
> inclining his head he said to himself: 'Wretched creatures,
> why did we give you to a mortal master, you who do not
> grow old or die? Was it so that you could share men's
> sorrows? There is no creature that breathes and crawls on
> earth more miserable than man.'
> *Iliad* XVII 434-47

Xanthos 1993/4
Ceramic and steel
70 × 12½ × 26½ in (177.5 × 32 × 67.5 cm)

24

THE ACHAIANS
Nestor
Νεστωρ

Nestor is King of Pylos in the Peloponnese and the most experienced of the Achaian leaders. He is too old now to play more than a token part in the actual fighting, but reminisces at length about the greater heroes he has known and the astounding deeds he himself has performed in the past. However, he is always accorded great respect in councils of war:

> Then Nestor rose to speak to them: the Pylians' spokesman was a persuasive and powerful orator and his voice flowed more sweetly than honey. He had already survived two generations of the men who had been born and grown up in his time in the sacred city of Pylos, and he ruled the third.
> *Iliad* 1 247-52

Nestor 1993/4
Ceramic, steel and jarrah wood
72 × 27½ × 17 in (183 × 70 × 43 cm)

25

THE ACHAIANS
Ajax   Αιας

Son of Telamon, King of the island of Salamis, and often called Telamonian Ajax or Ajax the Great to distinguish him from another, smaller Ajax. Ajax the Great is enormous and, in the absence of Achilles, is the Achaian hero chosen by lot to meet Hector in single combat:

> The giant Ajax, the Achaians' tower of defence, went out with a smile on his fierce face, walking with huge strides, brandishing and casting a great shadow with his spear. The Achaians' spirits rose at the sight of him, but a dreadful trembling gripped the joints of every Trojan and even Hector's heart thudded in his chest . . . Ajax, holding his fortress-wall of a shield — bronze over seven layers of hide — came nearer.
> *Iliad* VII 211-20

The fight ends in a chivalrous draw and Hector exchanges his sword for part of Ajax's armour.

Ajax 1993/4
Ceramic, steel, pine wood and jarrah wood
80½ × 18 × 23 in (204 × 46 × 58.5 cm)

26

THE ACHAIANS
Diomedes   Διομηδης

King of Argos, youngest and most dashing of the Greek heroes. After the withdrawal of Achilles, and until he himself has to withdraw with a wound, Diomedes takes the leading part in most of the battles and, spurred on by the goddess Athene, even attacks and wounds two of the gods helping the other side. One of the Trojan heroes says of Diomedes:

> '. . . a ferocious warrior and a dangerous agent of panic and rout, who in my opinion has now become the most formid-able of all the Achaians. Even the champion Achilles, who they say is the son of a goddess, never frightened us as much as this. The man fights like a madman, no one has the spirit to stand up to him.'
> *Iliad* VI 97-101

Diomedes 1993/4
Ceramic, oak wood and steel
80 × 15 × 16 in (203 × 38 × 41 cm)

27

THE ACHAIANS
Odysseus   Οδυσσευς

King of a distant island, he leads one of the smallest
contingents in the Achaian army. But, enjoying the special favour of
the goddess Athene, he is the cleverest and most enterprising of the
Achaian heroes. Furthermore, he is an eloquent speaker, a tough
fighter and, as he himself modestly claims (and demonstrates by winning prizes for wrestling, running and discus-throwing), 'I am not
bad, not at all bad at most kinds of athletics'. King Priam, looking
down from one of the towers of Troy at the enemy army drawn up
during a truce, asks Helen seated beside him:

> 'Now tell me, dear child, who is that? A head shorter
> than King Agamemnon, he looks broader across the chest
> and shoulders . . .'
> Helen, the daughter of Zeus, replied: 'That is the son of
> Laertes, cunning Odysseus; he grew up on the rocky island
> of Ithaca and is a master of every kind of trick and secret
> stratagem.'
> *Iliad* III 192-202

Odysseus 1993/4
Ceramic, jarrah wood, pine wood and steel
68 × 29 × 15 in (172 × 74 × 38 cm)

28

THE TROJANS
Mount Ida   Ἰδη

The gods live on Mount Olympos, on the Greek main-
land, but they obtain a closer view of the war from Ida, the sacred
mountain south of Troy. Its highest peak is called Gargaron:

> Zeus came to Ida, full of springs and home to wild
> creatures; he came to Gargaron, where incense is burnt on
> his own special altar . . . he seated himself on the summit
> exulting in his glory, looking out at the Trojans' city and
> the Achaians' ships.
> *Iliad* VIII 47-52

Mount Ida 1993/4
Ceramic and steel
36 × 49 × 21½ in (91.5 × 125 × 55 cm)

THE TROJANS
Helen   Ελενη

    The beautiful daughter of Zeus, wife of the King of Sparta,
Menelaos, until the goddess Aphrodite makes her fall in love with
Paris. In Troy, she and Paris are still lovers, King Priam is kind to
her and Hector polite, but she is isolated and unhappy, often wishing
she could go home with her husband or that she had died as soon
as she left Sparta.

    The Trojan elders sitting on the battlements saw Helen
come up onto the wall and chattered busily to one another:
'Hardly surprising the Trojans and Achaians should suffer
so much and so long for this woman – she looks like a
goddess, her face is astonishingly like an immortal's – even
so, whatever she may be, let her go away in the ships –
she's a catastrophe for us and our children – let her not
stay here!'
Iliad III 153–60

Helen 1993/4
Ceramic, bronze, brass and steel
62 × 22 × 20 in (157.5 × 56 × 51 cm)

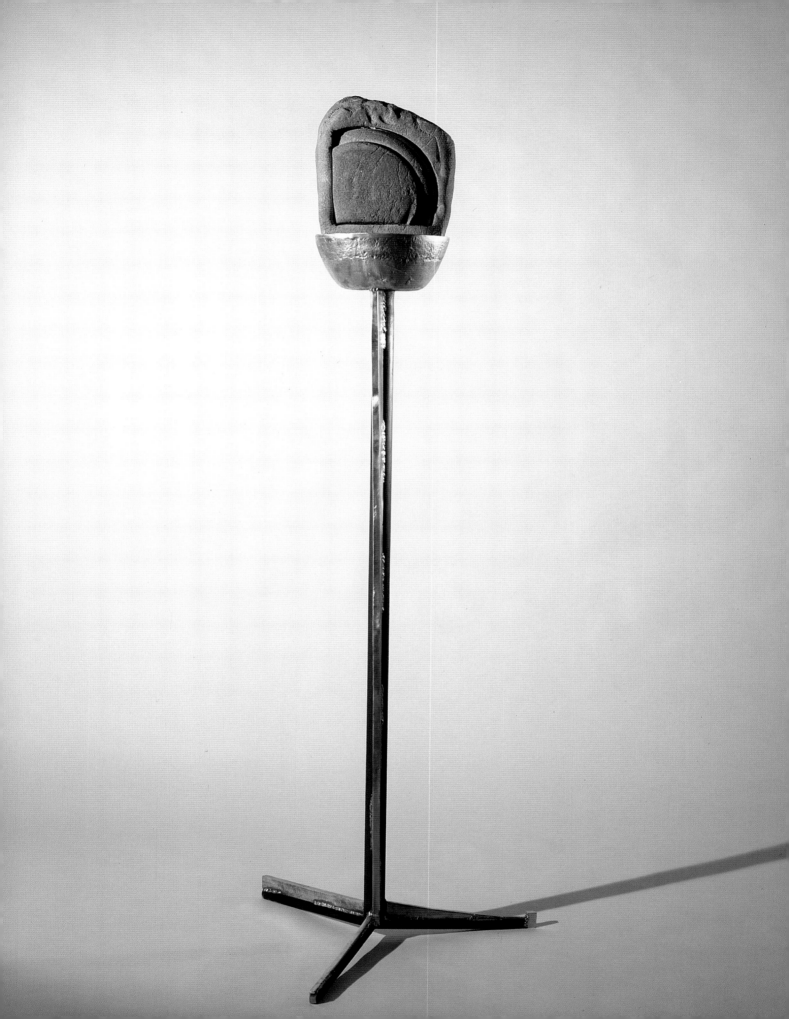

THE TROJANS
Paris   Παρις

Second son of King Priam of Troy, seducer of Helen. He
is not much liked by anyone – even on his own side – and Helen
herself abuses him, although she goes to bed with him immediately
afterwards. He is an excellent archer, wounding Diomedes and
eventually killing Achilles; but a bow is not considered a sufficiently
heroic weapon by these masters of the spear and sword and he takes
everything too lightly:

> Like a stallion which has eaten enough barley in the stable
> and – thinking of a bathe in the fast-flowing river – breaks
> its halter and gallops out on the plain, exulting; then, head
> high, mane streaming over both shoulders, magnificently
> pleased with himself, races for the pasture where they graze
> the mares; so Paris, his armour shining in the sun, ran
> down laughing from the citadel of Troy and caught up
> with noble Hector . . .
> 'My dear brother, you're in a hurry and I'm afraid my
> dawdling has delayed you – I didn't come exactly when
> you said.'
>   Hector, his helmet flashing, replied:
> 'You're a maniac! No reasonable man could despise what
> you do in battle – you are brave. Yet you're deliberately
> careless and never ready. It upsets me when I hear the
> Trojans – suffering so much on your account – talking
> about you with contempt.'
> *Iliad* VI 506-25

Paris 1993/4
Porcelain, stainless steel and steel
$67\frac{1}{2} \times 13 \times 14$ in ($172 \times 33 \times 36$ cm)

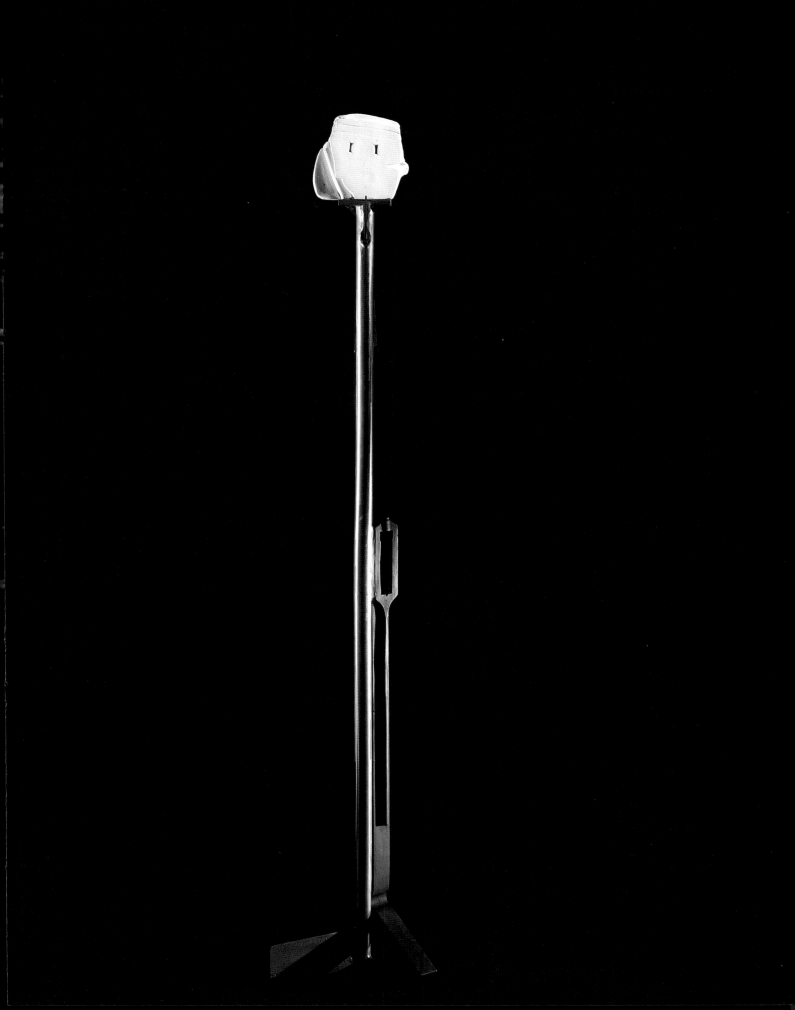

THE TROJANS
Hector   Εκτωρ

Eldest son of King Priam, he is the Trojans' champion
fighter as well as their commander-in-chief. He seems to be everywhere
on the battlefield, reinvigorating his troops and smiting down
Achaians. He leads the ferocious Trojan attack on the Greek camp,
which breaks through their rampart and almost succeeds in destroying
their ships. Hector is a more straightforward and immediately
sympathetic hero than the angry and vengeful Achilles and never more
so than when, having determined to face his terrible adversary alone
in front of Troy, he suddenly loses his nerve and runs away. After
being chased three times round the walls of Troy, he turns and fights,
but, with the gods against him, is swiftly killed.

Achilles pulled his bronze spear out of the body and laid
it down out of the way, then stripped the shoulders of their
bloody armour. Other Achaians came running up from all
around and stared at Hector's powerful and extraordinarily
beautiful corpse, but not one of them came near without
making a wound in it. Each would say, looking at the one
standing next to him: 'God, yes, Hector is a lot easier to
deal with now than when he set fire to the ships!' And
saying so, each would come up close and give him a
wound.
Iliad XXII 367-75

The Death of Hector 1993/4
Ceramic, pine wood and steel
66 × 48 × 53 in (168 × 122 × 135 cm)

32

THE TROJANS
Andromache   Ανδρομαχη

Wife of Hector. They have a small son called Astyanax who, in a famous scene when Hector takes leave of Andromache before going out to fight, is frightened by his father's helmet. Andromache is organising a hot bath for Hector's return when she hears shrieks from the city wall:

> She ran through the hall like a madwoman, her heart pounding – her attendants with her – and when she came to the wall and the crush of people, she stopped there on the battlement and looking all round suddenly saw him in front of the city, being dragged along: the chariot was dragging him rapidly and shamefully by his heels towards the Achaian ships. Black night covered her eyes, she fell backwards and lost her senses. Her splendid headdress was flung far away – the fillet and net, the plaited head-band and the veil given her by golden Aphrodite, that day when Prince Hector led her out of her father's house, after giving more gifts than could be counted.
> *Iliad* XXII 460-72

Andromache 1993/4
Ceramic and steel
57 × 24 × 17½ in (145 × 61 × 44.5 cm)

33

THE TROJANS
King Priam   Πριαμος

King of Troy, father of Hector, Paris and forty-eight other sons (nineteen by his wife Hecuba) as well as several daughters. After Hector's death he makes his way by night to visit the still relentless Achilles and beg for his son's body. Achilles does relent at last and they both sit down to a meal of mutton kebabs:

When they had eaten and drunk all they wanted, Priam sat admiring Achilles, his size, his presence: it was like looking at one of the gods. And Achilles sat admiring Priam, observing his noble appearance, impressed with the way he talked. When they had looked at each other long enough, the old man, royal Priam, was the first to speak: 'Let me have a bed now, dear sir, beloved of Zeus, as quickly as you can, so that I may have the pleasure of lying down and sleeping sweetly. The lids have never closed over my eyes since my son lost his life at your hands; I have been weeping continuously and thinking about my endless troubles and rolling in the filth of my palace courtyard. And I swallowed nothing. But now I have eaten food and let sparkling wine flow down my throat.'
Iliad XXIV 628-42

King Priam 1993/4
Ceramic, pine wood and steel
54 × 29 × 13½ in (137 × 74 × 34.5 cm)

34

THE TROJANS
Aeneas   Αινειας

Son of Aphrodite, goddess of love, and the mortal
Anchises, Aeneas is one of the principal Trojan heroes, but often
resentful. He complains of the gods' favouritism towards Achilles and
of being treated shabbily by his own side — Achilles taunts him with
wanting to replace his cousin Priam as King of Troy. In a much later
epic, the Roman poet Virgil's *Aeneid*, he escapes from the Sack of
Troy, sails to Italy and founds the Roman state. In Homer, the gods
clearly have some glorious future in mind for him and intervene several
times to save his life. Even the sea-god Poseidon — usually anti-Trojan
— whisks him away from a dangerous encounter with Achilles:

> 'Whenever you meet Achilles, you must draw off! Other-
> wise, in spite of your destiny, you will enter the house of
> Hades. But when Achilles has met his death, then you can
> take courage and fight with the best. No other Achaian
> will strip you of your armour.'
> *Iliad* XX 335-9

Aeneas 1993/4
Ceramic, jarrah wood and steel
68 × 19½ × 17½ in (173 × 50 × 44.5 cm)

35

THE TROJANS
Sarpedon   Σαρπηδων

Son of Zeus by the mortal Europa and leader of Troy's
allies from Lycia. When Patroclos is driving the Trojans back towards
Troy, Sarpedon intercepts him and creates an unhappy dilemma for
his immortal father watching from above:

> Sarpedon, with his weapons, jumped down from his
> chariot; and on the other side Patroclos, as soon as he saw
> him, leapt out of his; and, like two screeching vultures
> fighting with crooked claws and hooked beaks on a high
> crag, they rushed at each other with loud shouts. Seeing
> them, Zeus felt pity and spoke to Hera, his sister and wife:
> 'This is misery, misery for me! I love Sarpedon more than
> any other mortal and he is fated to be killed by Patroclos.
> My heart is split in two as I try to decide whether to snatch
> him away from this miserable battle while he is still alive
> and put him down in his own pleasant land of Lycia, or
> to kill him at the hands of Patroclos.'
> *Iliad* XVI 426-38

Hera, no friend either to Trojans or to her husband's illicit children,
argues for Sarpedon's death and Zeus sadly consents.

Sarpedon 1993/4
Ceramic, steel and oak wood
$64\frac{1}{2} \times 26 \times 17$ in ($164 \times 66 \times 43$ cm)

36

THE TROJANS
Dolon   Δολων

Son of a Trojan herald (an important official of the King's household), Dolon is ugly, rich and a good runner. When Hector asks for someone to spy on the sleeping Achaian camp, Dolon volunteers, but only after he has obtained from Hector the promise of a reward far beyond his worth: to be given the chariot and horses of Achilles when the Achaians are defeated. Unfortunately for this man with a sharp eye for the main chance, Odysseus and Diomedes have chosen the same night to spy on the Trojans and they meet and catch Dolon on the way. Terrified, he tells them everything they want to know, but Diomedes is ruthless:

> Dolon's large hand was about to touch Diomedes' chin to beg for mercy, but Diomedes hit him quickly with his sword clean across the neck and cut through both tendons. The man was still crying out as his head rolled in the dust. They took the weasel-skin cap off his head, his wolf-skin, his springy bow and his long spear; and Odysseus held them up in his hands and prayed to Athene, provider of spoils . . .
> *Iliad* x 454-61

Dolon 1993/4
Ceramic and steel
$61\frac{1}{2} \times 13\frac{1}{2} \times 15\frac{1}{2}$ in (156 × 35 × 39.5 cm)

37

THE TROJANS
Iphition   Ιφιτιων

An ally of the Trojans from Lydia in Asia Minor.

> Then Achilles, determined and irresistible, sprang at the
> Trojans with a terrible shout. The first one he killed was
> Iphition, a brave man and the leader of a large force. His
> father was a noble warrior, his mother a water-nymph, and
> he came from the fertile country below snow-capped
> Mount Tmolos. The hero Achilles went straight for him,
> threw his spear at the middle of his head and split the skull
> completely in two. Iphition fell violently . . . darkness
> spread over his eyes and the wheels of the Achaian chariots
> ran through him in the front line of battle.
> *Iliad* xx 381-95

The Felling of Iphition 1993/4
Ceramic and steel
25 × 40 × 57 in (63 × 102 × 145 cm)

84

THE TROJANS
The Towers of Ilion   Ιλιον οφρυοεσσα

Ilion – or in Latin Ilium – is another name for Troy. The
city stood on a rock about 60 feet high, rising straight out of the plain.

> . . . as if flames were licking the whole of towering Ilion
> up to its very top . . .
> *Iliad* XXII 410﹑11

The Towers of Ilion 1993/4
Ceramic and steel
79 × 71 × 41 in (200 × 180 × 104 cm)

List of Plates